# HOW I WENT TO THE OSCARS WITHOUT A TICKET

Thank-You Michele, for your support!

Dee Thompson 69th OSCARS

# HOW I WENT TO THE OSCARS WITHOUT A TICKET

*(A true life story by Dee Thompson)*

**To order additional copies of this book, contact:**
Xlibris Corporation
1-888-795-4274
www.Xlibris.com
Orders@Xlibris.com
49090

In loving memory of my mother
Mrs. Evelyn Mable Thompson

And loving appreciation of my children
Michael, Dwight, Amore' & Deshawn Thompson

I got the acting bug and moved to Los Angeles, California in 1996. You see I decided to do this after treading the acting waters on the East Coast first, back in North Carolina. I had acquired my SAG (Screen Actors Guild) card prior to heading over to Los Angeles to jump into the big acting pond. I received it on a regional commercial. After attending acting classes in New York and in the North and South Carolina Regions, I felt it was time to go to the big leagues. If I was going to be an actor then, I needed to go where the actors were, Hollywood, California.

The acting bug bit me so bad that I even worked part-time for the airlines in hope of making an audition out west if called by a LA Talent Agent or Casting Director. I had mailed out numerous letters and headshots to them hoping they would call me for an audition. I figured, since I worked for the airlines I could make a standby flight with a couple of day's notice of the audition place and time. The calls never came. So, I quit my job and headed to LA. I had a plan. I purchased a round-trip ticket just in case I had to return home immediately. I stayed at a run down hotel near the airport. I later found out that this area was known for drugs and prostitution. I had a plan to make it in this acting business. Everyday I pursued my new career. At first, I rented a car to make my rounds in this new city then, my funds got low so I started looking for a place to stay besides the hotel. I looked at some places in East LA. They were quite inexpensive in price but, I found out it was an area saturated with gang activity. It wasn't an area cut out for me. After searching the papers and my resources, I finally came upon a single room on 29th St. and Vermont Ave. The owner had this huge house. He was a very kind older gentleman. His name was Ralph. He had other people staying in the house also. I found out he was involved in the theatre and so was his wife for many years. She was off doing theatre in New York. He was very kind. I felt comfortable with him and the house. I signed a six months lease with him. I was now officially a resident of LA. I had my phone turned on. I still remember that ring. It was music to my ears.

Everyday I would go out and pass out my headshots and resume. Armed with my personal CD player I would listen to Anita Baker as I headed for the bus stop. She accompanied me everywhere. I would go up to a building and walk inside and look at the tenant listing and look for anything that looked like a film, television, agent office or anything that had to do with acting. I would catch the elevator up to the very top floor of the building and that's where I begin my trek. I would go door to door, floor to floor knocking and introducing myself. I asked them if they were a film or television company and if I could leave them a headshot and resume of me. Everyone I met was polite about my interaction with them. I met some very interesting people this way. I even met a guy who managed professional wrestlers and asked me if I wanted to get into the business.

I passed and said, "I'm pursuing an acting career."

I guess he figured since I was a big guy I would be good for wrestling. I continued my door to door adventure in search of work as an actor. I continued down the building floor by floor. I did this on many streets of Hollywood, Los Angeles and San Fernando Valley. I can remember the time I came across a porno video distributor in one of the buildings. It was in the San Fernando Valley. It was hot as hell that day. They thought I was one of their actors. You could see behind the desk in the back area. They had like a warehouse of all these VHS videos stacked on racks almost up to the ceiling.

When I saw what they were all about I said, "Thanks" and left.

I looked through the phonebook or any resource I had to search for an agent. I found the Carter Wright Agency on Hollywood Boulevard in Hollywood, California. I called them on the phone. Around the same time, I called a management agency by the name of American Artists in San Fernando Valley, California. Well, long story short, the gentleman at the Carter Wright Agency said for me to come in and give him a monologue and bring headshots with me. The management agency also wanted to see me. What a blessing it was to be called about acting representation. I went to the Carter Wright Agency in Hollywood and auditioned for this little old lovely lady who had been in the business for many years. Her husband was there also. June and Carter, they were a lovely couple. They continuously bickered back and forth with each other. They volleyed back and forth about what to get for lunch as she went out the door to pick something up. He mumbled and grumbled about his wife June for a few minutes. They truly had a love affair for each other. They were a cute couple. When she came back with the food, I did an improve Sprite commercial for her and a monologue. She gave me some tips and pointers about the business, things to do and what not to do.

Carter chimed in, "Don't chew too much gum, its not good for you."

I signed a contract with them. I had a Hollywood Agent. I was in the acting business.

A couple days later I arrived at the American Artists Management Agency in Sherman Oaks, California. This is where I met the beautiful Sharon Kelly. She was impressed with my resume and decided to take me on as a talent. She had represented some of the cast from the "Beverly Hillbillies Television Show." I found that impressive and besides she was nice and had big pretty eyes. We got along well from day one. She was very likable and straight forward about the business and what she could do for my career and what I had to do in this business partnership. I was blessed. In less than two weeks I had an agent and a manager in Hollywood, California.

I was truly blessed. I continued my search for acting jobs. I registered with the Extra Casting Agencies and begin doing background work. Background actors are the ones you see walking in the scene in the background, drinking coffee at restaurants, passing each other in an office, etc. They are acting in their respective positions and help make the scene complete. However, they don't speak in the scene or have any dialogue. They mouth their conversations silently. These background actors help paint a picture for the director and also sometime interact with the star actor. I had bills to pay. This gave me a chance to find out about the business from other actors perspective and a chance to see the seasoned pros do their thing up close and personal. I worked on this television show titled, "High Incident," starring Blair Underwood. When I wasn't working background, I was looking for acting jobs and passing out my headshots and resumes. I was going door-to-door and giving them to any and everyone that would take them. I also walked through numerous studios going door-to-door passing out my credentials. I met quite a few people both, famous and not. I met Editors, 1$^{st}$ Ad's, 2$^{nd}$ Ad's, directors, gaffers, anyone that would give me their ear for a moment to introduce myself and let them know that I was looking for work as an actor. At the end of the day I was exhausted.

Everyday I returned to my small room at the boarding house. At night time you could hear and see the helicopters flying overhead and chasing the bad guys outside. The light would sometimes shine through my window. Everybody called them ghetto birds, because they were flying around in the ghetto chasing criminals. On the days when I had worked as a background extra, I came home with food that was given to me from the set. They were throwing it away in the garbage.

I saw this happen one day and I asked, "Why are you throwing all that food in the garbage can?", and the guy said, because they couldn't keep it.

He said something about them being liable if they kept it and used it again. He let me take what I wanted. This is when I started carrying a backpack, so I could take food home with me if they threw it out. My food bill literally disappeared when I was working background. Otherwise, it was those ten for a dollar pack of noodles that I ate so much of. Tuna in the can was also a bargain favorite. A couple of times things got real rough for me financially and I can remember not having soap to take a bath with. I had this small travel bottle of soap that was empty. I used it to refill in the bathrooms from nice hotels or wherever there was nice fresh liquid soap. That silky smooth soap, like Dove soap worked best to take a bath with. It wasn't irritating to my skin. I didn't want to steal. I was just trying to survive and make it. I only had a bus pass at the time and no money. God please forgive me.

I remember everyday when I would get off the bus at 29th and Vermont Avenue.; I would always see these helicopters flying around in the sky in circles. I thought it was pretty cool. I served at a helicopter squadron back when I was in the United States Navy. It brought back some great memories of serving in the military. I love helicopters and airplanes.

I asked my neighbor one day, "Why are all those helicopters flying around in the sky all the time?" he said, "The Oscars is being held over there."

I said, "The Oscars? You mean for like acting?"

He said, "Yeah, they have it right over there, a couple of streets over at the Shrine Auditorium."

I thought to myself, "Wow, that's cool, the Oscars."

I begin to think to myself, "What actor wouldn't mind going to the Oscars, either to view it or to be receiving it."

I started to daydream. If I could go to the Oscars that would be a dream come true for me. That night I went home with this on my mind. I grew up in Charlotte, North Carolina. My mother was an evangelist minister. We always stayed in church, ever since I was little. We went to many churches big and small. I remember going to a small church were the minister was just starting out and he had this small rickety building and it had no heat in it. This place looked like it was about to fall in. It was in the winter time and it was extremely cold outside. He had this oil or wood heater, I can't remember which, but it took a while to warm up in there. I remember me and my younger brother Lee volunteering to play the drums just so that we could stay warm. Eventually, the Holy Ghost got in there and the lord moved his blessings on us. It was warm then. Those were some good times.

My mother used to always say, "Be careful what you ask God for because you just might get it, he can answer all prayers. Just pray and ask him for what you want."

That night before I went to bed I prayed," Dear lord please let me go to the Oscars."

I heard a sound respond in spirit say, "Prepare yourself and go."

I knew it was God speaking to me to answer my prayer. I went to sleep and had a great deep sleep, man I slept good. The next day when I woke up I continued to pursue my acting career. As I looked for jobs and passed out my headshots, I begin to tell people that I was going to the Oscars. **This day was different**. Since I was going to the Oscars, I had to prepare myself and get ready for the big day. First, I found out what day it was going to be on. I didn't own a tuxedo. I had a double breasted black suit. I had to put it in the cleaners to be cleaned. I did that. I figured also, if I was going to the Oscars then, I want to take some pictures to keep as memories. So, I caught the bus over to the K-mart on 3<sup>rd</sup> Street and purchased a small portable camera. I think I paid about seven or eight dollars for it. A couple days later, I picked up my double breasted black suit from the cleaners. I was ready to go. I rode the bus home. I got home and took a bath and put on my suit. I took my portable camera and put it in my front suit pocket on the left. I left the house.

I walked down the steps out the back door of my boarding house on my way to the Oscars. I walked down the sidewalk. It was a beautiful day outside. As I walked down the sidewalk, I spoke to people in the neighborhood sitting on their porches relaxing. They kind of stared at me as I passed them. I always try to speak to people in passing. That's how I was raised. As I got closer to the auditorium, I crossed the street and came upon a parking lot that had all these limos in it. There had to be about a hundred black and white limos parked there. One of them had the door open and a guy was just sitting there in the seat with the door open. I've always admired limos. I asked him how was he doing and where did all these limos come from?

He said, "These are parked here from the event at the Shrine Auditorium."

I said, "That's cool, can you take a picture of me getting out of one?"

He said, "Yeah sure," so I took out my camera and handed it to him.

I changed places with him and sat in the seat where he had been sitting. I had the door open and acted like I was getting out of the limousine. He took the picture. I thanked him and moved on.

As I got closer to the building I saw this big guy, (I can't remember his name) we had done some background work together on a movie, I think it was "Bulworth." The movie starred Warren Beatty, Halle Berry, Isiah Washington, Don Cheadle, Oliver Platt, Michael Clarke Duncan and many others. I had finished working on the television show "High Incident" late one night and was returning home from shooting in Sun Valley, California. As I got close to my house I saw some film trucks parked alongside the curb. Film trucks are always parked around the city shooting different productions. I figured since it was close to the house where I lived then, I would stop and see what was going on. You see, I always continued to pass out my headshots looking for new work and besides, that was my last day on "High Incident."

As I slowed to park my rental car I asked the security guard, "What are they shooting?"

I needed the rental to get out to the remote location in Sun Valley.

He said, "They're shooting a movie."

I asked, "What's the name of it and who's in it?"

He said, "The name of the movie is "Bulworth" or something like that and "I don't know who's in it."

I parked the small rental car and walked up to him to ask some more questions about the filming crew and could I go up and leave a headshot with the 1st AD (First Assistant Director), UPM, (Unit Production Manager) or one of the PA's (Production Assistants). The film industry has a language all their own. They've shortened the long titles of the jobs. It's almost like speaking code sometimes. It makes you feet a part of the industry when you can talk like this.

He said, "Yeah man, go ahead, do your thang."

It was about 3 o'clock in the morning. It was kinda foggy and misty outside.

Anyway, I walked up on the set and I saw Isiah Washington. I know who he is now but, I didn't know who he was back then. I introduced myself and asked him about the film.

He said, "It's a movie starring Warren Beatty, Halle Berry . . . ,"

I said, "Halle Berry?"

He said, "Yeah, she's in it and plays the girl that Warren Beatty is trying to get with; in the film. She's sitting right around there."

He pointed in a direction around the corner of a trailer.

He said, "Go around there and talk to her, she'll show you some love."

So, I walked around the corner of the trailer with my headshots in my hand and there she was; sitting there chillin, all by herself. I introduced myself. The conversation went something like this as I reached out to shake her hand.

"Hi! I'm Dee Thompson, I'm from Charlotte, North Carolina and I'm out here pursuing an acting career. I admire your work. Is there anyway possible I can work on this film?"

She said, "Well, everything's been cast already but, you might be able to work background as an extra or something. "I tell you what, call this number tomorrow and she might be able to help."

The number was for a Casting Director by the name of Victoria Thomas, who I know today by the name as Vicki Thomas, one of Hollywood's biggest Casting Directors. I called Vicki Thomas the next day and she was real polite.

I told her, "I met Halle Berry yesterday on the set of "Bulworth" and she told me to call you." I explained I was looking for work as an actor.

She said, "All the principle roles have been filled already but, if you want to work as an extra, I might be able to get you in. Call Teresa Smith, her number is . . ."

I hung up the phone and called Teresa Smith and explained the situation and she said, "I tell you what, I probably could use you as my Henchman Number Two. Report to the set tomorrow and when you check in ask for me."

The next day I reported to this abandoned night club on Hollywood Boulevard where they were shooting. I checked in with the PA and asked to speak to Teresa Smith, the Extra's Casting Director. She checked off my name on the list and gave me a SAG (Screen Actors Guild) Extra's Voucher. I was directed to go to wardrobe and get dressed. I was outfitted as a big bouncer type. Doo rag, black shirt, black pants, (I still have them-they gave them to me), dark shades, gold chains, the works. After I finished getting dressed, I reported to the set for the club scene.

Teresa saw me and said, "Great! Come with me."

She took me over to see Mr. Warren Beatty himself. He took a good look at me and said, "Yeah, he'll do," or something to that effect. I later found out that Mr. Beatty wrote, was directing and acting in the film. It was a trip seeing him do that. He had to cut himself. When the director yells, "cut" the scene ends. After I was cleared for his approval

Teresa said, "Just hang out here for a while till they get ready for you."
As I was walking back to the seating area for the extras I saw Halle Berry.
I said, "Thanks for your help, everything worked out."
She smiled and said, "See, I told ya!"
She left and went to the set. I was truly grateful. She reminded me of my cute little niece named Terrica, my brother's daughter. Halle was so cute and innocent, fragile but, cute. She was pretty as hell, now that I could see her in the daylight. That's how I met Halle Berry. Getting back to my trip to the Oscars and meeting the big Samoan guy that I had worked with on "Bulworth."

He saw me walking up and he said, "Heh man, what's up? I see you doing big things."

I said, "Yeaaah man," gave him some dap (handshake), a breast to breast hug and told him to take care.

Look like he was guarding a door or something or maybe waiting on somebody. He was dressed in a black tuxedo.

I continued my walk to the Oscars. I came upon some people that were standing behind a barricade on the sidewalk. I think they were from Australia or somewhere overseas. They had an accent. They asked me, who was I and was I going to the Oscars?

**HERE I AM BEHIND THE BARRICADE ACROSS THE STREET FROM THE SHRINE AUDITORIUM**
**(Notice the 69TH Annual Academy Awards sign on the Shrine Auditorium)**

I told them, "My name is Dee Thompson and I'm an actor, I'm out here pursuing an acting career."

They immediately asked for my autograph and we took some pictures. It was cool. I remember one of the younger teenage girls in the group ask me, if I knew Leonardo DiCaprio? I told her no that I had never met him but, that would be cool if I did. This other guy came up to me and started talking. He was a black guy and he looked like he was a musician or a singer from one of the old R&B groups, like someone from the James Brown band or something. He asked for an autograph. I gave it to him. We also took a picture. We were directly across the street from the entrance to the Shrine Auditorium. Right in front of us limos were pulling up and letting people out to go down the red carpet into the Shrine Auditorium. All types of celebrity people were getting out. I took pictures also like everyone else from across the street. I had someone take pictures with my camera of the folks I was talking with behind the barrier. I wanted to capture these memories of me meeting these folks. This was cool.

All of a sudden a voice spoke to me and said, "Go up and go across the street to the other side."

So, I did it. I crossed the street a ways up away from all the hoopla and came down on the other side of the street on the sidewalk. Now, I was on the side were all the limos were pulling up. Of course there was a crowd of people on that side of the street also. I just came up to the crowd and like everyone else was taking in the moment. The cars continuously filed in one after another back-to-back pulling up to the red carpet and dropping the celebrities and their entourages off on the red carpet. The light bulbs were flashing. This was a major thing happening. Everybody was screaming somebody's name as the people got out of the car. As they exited the cars, they waved, blew kisses, etc. to the crowd and walked in.

There was a gentleman standing in front of me with a ponytail hanging down his back. He had on a black tuxedo and was standing there like I was. We were part of the crowd and being held back by security and police who controlled the event. We were just standing there looking at what was happening. Once again, a voice spoke to me (I'll say it was God), because this is who I prayed to and asked this for. He said, "Speak some Italian to this guy." I had served my country in the U.S. Navy on active duty and was stationed in Italy for a few years. There, I learned to speak Italian. So, I spoke to the gentleman in Italian.

I said, "Hi! How are you doing and are you Italian?" I continued, "I used to live in Italy for a while, my name is Dee Thompson."

He responded in Italian and said, "Ciao! What's Up Man? I saw you earlier; didn't you come in with Eddie Murphy and them? I thought I saw you guys getting out of the car."

Before I could answer, he continued to speak. You know how there are people when they ask you a question, that they answer it before you can speak? Then, this was one of those guys. He would not let me get a word in edgewise.

I was just able to say, "Yeah, un huh." Because, when I tried to explain to him it wasn't me in my slow Italian, he basically made it me. So, I just kept saying, "Yeah, un huh." Everything happened so quick he didn't give me much room to explain myself and who I was. However, we immediately became friends. I felt as if I had known him for many years. I felt a connection to this guy somehow. Damn! He was chatty. I was still trying to see who was getting out of the cars pulling up.

He then turned and looked at me and said in English, "Heh man you goin in?"

I said, "Yeah", so we proceeded right around the crowd past the police and security to the red carpet entrance. I followed him. As we walked right past the policemen and big tough security guys with ear pieces in their ears, the crowd continued to scream out different names of people.

We walked down the red carpet between the bleachers of screaming fans and admirers. They screamed, waved and pointed. I waved back at them. It was a cool, quite electrifying feeling walking down this bright red carpet. It was like being at a football game or something and you were the home team coming out. I waved and smiled. This was exciting. My friend and I continued past the flashing cameras and press people taking pictures and holding their microphones. This was a trip. Everybody had on black. Black gowns, black shoes, black tuxedos; imagine that, in sunny LA. It was cool though. It didn't matter, I was at the Oscars. I didn't know any of these people personally. It was kinda like a surfer being on a big black wave and just being pushed and sucked in by this ocean of black contrasting against the red. I just rode the wave as we were being heralded toward the Shrine Auditorium Building. As we got closer to the building I could see for the very first time in my life what the building looks like where they have the Oscars at. This was a beautiful magnificent building. It was absolutely beautiful to me. They had it all decked out with a sign at the top that read:

# 69th ANNUAL ACADEMY AWARDS.

We continued toward the entrance to the building. Let me tell you, they had all types of security there. They probably still had the helicopters flying overhead but, I didn't hear them at this time. I was caught up in all the commotion of the Oscars. At the entrance to the building they had security wands and physical searches. People were emptying their pockets and showing their passes; you name it. Security was present and accounted for. However, we just walked right into the building past the barrage of security and everyone. This is how I know a higher being was in charge of the evening. They didn't even ask me or my new found friend for anything or acknowledge us at all. We just walked right through the doors as if no one was there at all. Once inside, I saw all these beautiful flowers everywhere. They had decorated the building inside also. It was a grand night to behold. Once inside, I immediately noticed Dennis Rodman the basketball player was there.

I went over extended my hand and introduced myself. "What's Up Man," I'm Dee, Dee Thompson."

Dennis said," What's up?" We both proceeded over to the bar they had setup in the lobby foyer area. He ordered a beer and I ordered a Sprite with lemon.

I went to pay for both drinks and he said, "I got it."

I told him he was a great basketball player and that I played against James Worthy growing up in high school back in North Carolina.

He smiled and said, "Thanks."

**NBA BASKETBALL GREAT DENNIS RODMAN
TALKING TO ADMIRERS AT THE 69th ANNUAL ACADEMY AWARDS**

After we received our drinks he went back into the auditorium and I went back over to where my friend Norm Vincelli was standing.

Norm said, "You ready?"

I said, "Yeah, let's go."

I followed him inside the theater. The place was packed. He walked to an aisle and we proceeded past seated guest to two empty seats. This guy had a seat for me to sit down. There were other people there that knew him also. He introduced them to me. They were nice and wanted to know if I was nominated for something. I told them no. He was telling them that I was with Eddie Murphy or something to that effect. I couldn't quite hear him whispering to the other people what he was saying. Besides, I was too busy looking around and watching the other actors, producers, special effects people and others that were in the same industry as I. The band begins to play.

Billy Crystal was the Host. I saw Cuba Gooding, Jr. receive his Oscar. Man, he was excited. I would have been too. Tom Cruise was there also. Cuba received his Oscar for his work in the "Jerry McGuire" movie. Show me the money. I loved that movie. Billy Bob Thornton also received an Oscar for his work in his film "Sling blade." Michael Kidd was presented an Honorary Oscar in recognition of his services to the Art of the Dance in the Art of the Screen. Jim Carey was there, Will Smith, Julie Andrews, Tommy Lee Jones, Glenn Close, Al Pacino, Bette Midler, Nicolas Cage, Jeffrey Rush from "Shine"; and Frances McDormand from the movie "Fargo" and so many others. The place was packed with movie stars. Madonna sang "You Must Love Me," Kenny Loggins "For The First Time," Celine Dion "Because You Loved Me," and Natalie Cole and Arturo Sandoval "I Finally Found Someone." As I looked around the room, I saw so many faces that I had watched for years at the movie theaters and on television. **I was at the Oscars.** The rest of the award ceremony went in a blur. It went too fast. There was so much going on I could hardly consume it all. It's like I wanted to put it in slow mo, so I could remember it all. Between Norm asking me questions and me trying to see everything, I got lost in the event and it was hard to maintain focus. There was also these station commercial breaks were they gave the audience a break to run out, take care of business and get back to their assigned seats. They announced how far away they were to coming back live on the air.

"Back in two minutes, please everyone take your seats", the announcer said.

They came back, announced the remaining winners, including "Best Picture," then it was over, just like that.

Everybody hugged and congratulated each other and the crowd begin to file out of the auditorium. Me and Norm walked around the auditorium and up to the stage. I took out my disposal camera I had bought at K-Mart and begin taking pictures of everything. I took one of him standing on the steps of the stage, he took one of me. I was standing in front of the security guys on the stage. I even took one on the stage behind the podium. It was fun taking pictures on the stage where everyone had just received their Oscars. The security guys gave us carte blanch for our little photo shoot. After we snapped a few more photos we proceeded out into the lobby.

Norm said, "Hey, we're going over to the Vanity party, you need a ride over there?"

I said, "No, go ahead I'll probably see you over there later, I'ma stick around here for a few."

We exchanged numbers and parted our different ways. I went back inside the auditorium. I met Raul Julia, Jr., and his lady friend. He is the son of the famous actor Raul Julia from the "Adams Family" movie. We begin to talk about the award show. He was real cool. He talked a little about his dad. His dad was a great actor and funny as hell. I was taking in the architecture of the inside of the building and looked up at the ceiling and noticed this beautiful chandelier overhead. I showed it to them. We stood there looking up at the ceiling at this chandelier in the Shrine Auditorium. It was beautiful. We enjoyed the moment. We talked about one day being up there on the stage receiving an Oscar ourselves. We dreamed together and laughed about it. He signed my Oscar program book. We shook hands and said it was nice meeting each other. We parted our separate ways.

**HERE I AM STANDING ON THE STEPS OF THE STAGE AT THE 69TH ANNUAL ACADEMY AWARDS SHOW**
*(Notice the Security Guys In The Background With The Earpieces)*

**THE FRONT STAGE OF THE 69ᵀᴴANNUAL ACADEMY AWARDS
SHOW WITH SECURITY GUARDS POSTED ON THE STEPS
AFTER THE SHOW**

**THE BEAUTIFUL STAGE SETTING OF THE 69TH ANNUAL ACADEMY AWARDS SHOW WITH THE PODIUM IN THE BACKGROUND WHERE PRESENTERS ANNOUNCED THE WINNERS**

I again, left the auditorium and went out into the lobby area. I saw people going into this room next door, so I went over to see what was going on. People was milling around talking and laughing. I saw a huge statute of a gold Oscar there. I asked a bystander if they could take a picture of me standing beside it. They took the picture. I saw Billy Bob Thornton come out with his Oscar in his hand.

I told him, "Congratulations, that was a great movie, can I take a picture with you?"

He said, "Sure," so I asked another bystander to take the picture for me.

We held the Oscar between us. I thanked him. As I begin to take more photos, the official press people begin to start shooting photos also.

The security guys intervened and said, "No photos please." However, they let me continue to take my pictures and greet everyone coming into the area. God was at work. I took a picture with Rick Baker. He did makeup for many celebrities in the business. His credits includes "The Grinch," starring Jim Carey, "The Nutty Professor," starring Eddie Murphy, "Planet of the Apes," starring Michael Clarke Duncan and many, many other films. He can transform an actor into a totally different being.

**DEE THOMPSON AND RICK BAKER STRIKE A POSE TOGETHER
AFTER THE 69th ANNUAL ACADEMY AWARDS SHOW**
(*Rick Baker was awarded the OSCAR "For Achievement In Makeup" for the
film "The Nutty Professor" starring Eddie Murphy*)

**A SAFETY SHOT WITH "THE MASTER OF MAKEUP", MR. RICK BAKER AND DEE THOMPSON**
(*Notice my Double-Breasted Suit with my Tuxedo Shirt*)

**POSING WITH MR.OSCAR AFTER THE "69<sup>TH</sup> ANNUAL
ACADEMY AWARDS SHOW"
IN THE LOBBY OF THE SHRINE AUDITORIUM JUST
OUTSIDE THE GOVERNOR'S BALLROOM**

A lady came up to me and asked did I get a program book.

I said, "No." She then led me over to this table were they were. She handed me a green hardback book that was wrapped in cellophane plastic wrap.

There was music coming from down the hall and I asked her, "What band is that playing in there" and she said, she didn't know. She said it was the Governors Ball. I walked back there to take a peek. As I walked in I was directed to a seating area by a gentleman. There was a band playing and people were dancing. On the table was a small cake with a small chocolate Oscar on top of it. They served me food. I ate and enjoyed the music. They had these pink napkins. I took the pink napkin and wrapped the chocolate Oscar in it to eat later on. I didn't even dance. I love to dance. I sat there and enjoyed the evening. The music was wonderful and everybody looked beautiful. I just looked around the room. As it got later in the night, I decided it was time to go and let the Cinderella night come to an end. I got up and walked across the dance floor with my chocolate Oscar in my napkin, my 69th Oscar Program and my green hard back book that was wrapped in plastic and headed for the exit the same way that I came in. The crowd was thinning out now. Everyone was filing out, down the corridors of the hallway and back out through the huge doors, across the red carpet the same way that they came in. Back past, the now empty bleachers and to the waiting limousines pulling up to whisk them away to other late night parties and to take them home.

As I was standing there, waiting for things to clear out, a lady standing close by me asked, "Do you have a ride?"

I said, "no."

She said, "well my ride will be here in a moment, if you want to ride with me you can." "There's a couple of us riding together."

I said, "Sure, I'd love to." I introduced myself.

Just then, her limo pulled up. She said, "Here we go" and walked to get into the limousine. I followed her.

Once inside the car, there were other people already in the car.

I spoke and said, "Hi" to them and she said, "This is my friend Dee, he's just getting a ride with us. Where are you going?"

I said, "You can drop me off right around the corner, I just live down the street."

I directed the driver to my neighborhood. The trip was short and quick, about three blocks quick. The limo pulled up in front of the big boarding house.

I thanked her and everyone in the limo and said, "Take care, you guys have fun, it was a pleasure meeting you." I opened the door and got out.

The car pulled off into the darkness. I walked around the side of the house to the entrance to my place and walked up the tiny stairs in the back. I opened the door and stepped inside. I put my chocolate Oscar wrapped up in the pink napkin in the tiny refrigerator. I took off my double-breasted coat and threw it on the bed.

I then, looked up at the ceiling and I said, **"Thank you God, thank-you"** and I lifted up my hands toward the ceiling and begin to cry uncontrollably and praising his holy name, thanking him for the miracle that had just happened to me. I was overcome with joy and emotion. I had just been to the Oscars.

MARTY
PATTON
HAMLET
BEN-HUR
ROCKY
WINGS
GIGI
ANNIE HALL
GOING MY WAY
AN AMERICAN IN PARIS
A MAN FOR ALL SEASONS
IN THE HEAT OF THE NIGHT
HOW GREEN WAS MY VALLEY
IT HAPPENED ONE NIGHT
MUTINY ON THE BOUNTY
TERMS OF ENDEARMENT
FROM HERE TO ETERNITY
GENTLEMAN'S AGREEMENT
THE LOST WEEKEND
ALL THE KING'S MEN
CHARIOTS OF FIRE
ALL ABOUT EVE
MY FAIR LADY
GRAND HOTEL
THE GODFATHER
SCHINDLER'S LIST
ORDINARY PEOPLE
THE LAST EMPEROR
WEST SIDE STORY
OUT OF AFRICA
FORREST GUMP
CASABLANCA
TOM JONES
CIMARRON
MRS. MINIVER
UNFORGIVEN
CAVALCADE
RAIN MAN
THE STING
OLIVER!
AMADEUS
PLATOON
REBECCA
GANDHI
BRAVEHEART
THE LIFE OF EMILE ZOLA
MIDNIGHT COWBOY
ON THE WATERFRONT
THE SILENCE OF THE LAMBS
AROUND THE WORLD IN 80 DAYS
THE BEST YEARS OF OUR LIVES
LAWRENCE OF ARABIA
THE BRIDGE ON THE RIVER KWAI
YOU CAN'T TAKE IT WITH YOU
THE FRENCH CONNECTION
ALL QUIET ON THE WESTERN FRONT
THE GREATEST SHOW ON EARTH
ONE FLEW OVER THE CUCKOO'S NEST
DRIVING MISS DAISY ★ THE SOUND OF MUSIC
THE GODFATHER PART II ★ KRAMER VS. KRAMER
GONE WITH THE WIND ★ THE APARTMENT
DANCES WITH WOLVES ★ THE DEER HUNTER
THE GREAT ZIEGFELD ★ THE BROADWAY MELODY
**69TH ANNUAL ACADEMY AWARDS** ®

BOARD OF GOVERNORS BALL ★ MONDAY, MARCH 24, 1997

## MY FOOD STAINED PROGRAM FROM THE BOARD OF GOVERNORS BALL

**GOVERNORS BALL PROGRAM
FROM THE 69TH ANNUAL ACADEMY AWARDS SHOW**

This
ball is dedicated to those who have been nominated
for the 69th Annual Academy Awards,
and to the Honorary Award recipients
who have been honored by the
Board of Governors of the
Academy of Motion
Picture Arts and
Sciences.

## THE LIST OF HONOREES

### THOSE BEING HONORED AT THIS BALL ARE:

BRYAN ADAMS
JOAN ALLEN
DAVID LEROY ANDERSON
RICHARD L. ANDERSON
BUB ASMAN
LAUREN BACALL
RICK BAKER
BOB BEEMER
ANNA BEHLMER
ANNE BELLE
BILL W. BENTON
MARK BERGER
JULIETTE BINOCHE
BRENDA BLETHYN
KENNETH BRANAGH
BRIGITTE BROCH
JAMES L. BROOKS
PAUL BROWN
BEN BURTT
ALEX BYRNE
CHERYL CARASIK
CHRIS CARPENTER
BERNADETTE CARRANZA
SIMON CHANNING-WILLIAMS
ETHAN COEN
JOEL COEN
RICHARD CONDIE
STUART CRAIG
CAMERON CROWE
TOM CRUISE
CZECH REPUBLIC
ANTONELLO DE LEO
ROGER DEAKINS
DEBORAH LA MIA DENAVER
CALEB DESCHANEL
DEBORAH DICKSON
PATRICK DOYLE
SUSAN W. DRYFOOS
VOLKER ENGEL
STEFEN FANGMEIER

RALPH FIENNES
MILOS FORMAN
FRANCE
DAVID FRANKEL
JOHN FRAZIER
JUAN CARLOS FRESNADILLO
JUD J. FRIEDMAN
JAKE GARBER
LEON GAST
GEORGIA
ANGUS GIBSON
ELLIOT GOLDENTHAL
RICK GOLDSMITH
CUBA GOODING, JR.
GERRY HAMBLING
MARVIN HAMLISCH
WOODY HARRELSON
TIM HARVEY
BARBARA HERSHEY
SCOTT HICKS
DAVID HIRSCHFELDER
TIMOTHY HITTLE
JOHN HODGE
JAMES NEWTON HOWARD
JOE HUTSHING
RODERICK JAYNES
MARIANNE JEAN-BAPTISTE
ANDERS THOMAS JENSEN
BARRY JOSSEN
PIP KARMEL
DIANE KEATON
DARIUS KHONDJI
MICHAEL KIDD
HENRY LA BOUNTA
GREGG LANDAKER
ROBERT "MUTT" LANGE
MIKE LEIGH
ANDREW LLOYD WEBBER
PETER LORD
WILLIAM H. MACY

## THE LIST OF HONOREES

THOSE BEING HONORED AT THIS BALL ARE:

KIM MAGNUSSON
LAURENCE MARK
CATHERINE MARTIN
JEFFREY MARVIN
STEVE MASLOW
FRANCES McDORMAND
STEPHENIE McMILLAN
JO MENELL
CHRIS MENGES
ALAN MENKEN
ARTHUR MILLER
ANTHONY MINGHELLA
TYRON MONTGOMERY
BRIAN MORRIS
ARMIN MUELLER-STAHL
MATTHEW W. MUNGLE
WALTER MURCH
ALAN ROBERT MURRAY
RUTH MYERS
ANDY NELSON
CHRIS NEWMAN
RANDY NEWMAN
EDWARD NORTON
NORWAY
KEVIN O'CONNELL
DAVID PARKER
GEOFFREY PATTERSON
JANET PATTERSON
CHRIS PETERSON
CLAY PINNEY
RACHEL PORTMAN
NICK REDMAN
TIM RICE
ALLAN DENNIS RICH
ANN ROTH
GEOFFREY RUSH
GREG P. RUSSELL
RUSSIA
RICHARD SAKAI
JAN SARDI

JOHN SAYLES
ADAM SCHLESINGER
STEPHEN SCHWARTZ
JANE SCOTT
KRISTIN SCOTT THOMAS
JOHN SEALE
PAUL SEYDOR
MARC SHAIMAN
BAYLEY SILLECK
SUSANNE SIMPSON
DOUGLAS SMITH
DAVID SONENBERG
SCOTT SQUIRES
BRUCE STAMBLER
THOMAS STELLMACH
JAMES STRAUS
BARBRA STREISAND
BILLY BOB THORNTON
PHIL TIPPETT
PHILIPPE TURLURE
ANTONIO URRUTIA
JOSEPH VISKOCIL
DIANE WARREN
EMILY WATSON
BO WELCH
KIT WEST
KEITH A. WESTER
MICHAEL WESTMORE
KEN WESTON
JEFF WEXLER
SCOTT WHEELER
DAVID A. WHITTAKER
JOHN WILLIAMS
PERRY WOLFF
JAMES WOODS
GABRIEL YARED
JESSICA YU
SAUL ZAENTZ
HABIB ZARGARPOUR
HANS ZIMMER

## OFFICERS OF THE ACADEMY

\*\*\*

### ARTHUR HILLER
*President*

### SID GANIS
*First Vice President*

### ARTHUR HAMILTON
*Vice President*

### FAY KANIN
*Vice President*

### ROBERT REHME
*Treasurer*

### RODDY McDOWALL
*Secretary*

### BRUCE DAVIS
*Executive Director*

\*\*\*

## THE HEAVY WEIGHTS THAT MADE THE 69TH OSCARS SHOW HAPPEN

### *BOARD OF GOVERNORS*

\*\*\*

| | |
|---|---|
| DEDE ALLEN | KATHLEEN KENNEDY |
| JOHN BAILEY | HOWARD W. KOCH |
| CURT R. BEHLMER | MARVIN LEVY |
| CARL BELL | WILLIAM C. LITTLEJOHN |
| CHARLES BERNSTEIN | CAROL LITTLETON |
| ROBERT F. BOYLE | KARL MALDEN |
| BRUCE BROUGHTON | MARVIN MARCH |
| ALLEN DAVIAU | ROGER L. MAYER |
| LINWOOD G. DUNN | RODDY McDOWALL |
| RICHARD EDLUND | DONALD O. MITCHELL |
| JUNE FORAY | GREGORY PECK |
| JOHN FRANKENHEIMER | DANIEL PETRIE, JR. |
| SID GANIS | ROBERT REHME |
| DON HALL | BILL TAYLOR |
| ARTHUR HAMILTON | FRANK J. URIOSTE |
| ARTHUR HILLER | LEW R. WASSERMAN |
| CHERYL BOONE ISAACS | HASKELL WEXLER |
| NORMAN JEWISON | ALBERT WOLSKY |
| FAY KANIN | RICHARD D. ZANUCK |
| HAL KANTER | |

\*\*\*

## *ACKNOWLEDGEMENTS*

\*\*\*

BALL CATERED BY WOLFGANG PUCK
IN ASSOCIATION WITH RESTAURANT ASSOCIATES

BALL DECOR BY AMBROSIA PRODUCTIONS
FEATURING ARTIST HIRO YAMAGATA

MUSIC PROVIDED BY JACK SHELDON
AND THE JACK SHELDON ORCHESTRA
AND BY THE CHUCK WANSLEY BAND FEATURING
ELLIS HALL, JOY BURNWORTH AND GAVIN CHRISTOPHER

WINES COURTESY OF DON & RHONDA CARANO
OF FERRARI-CARANO VINEYARDS AND WINERY

CHAMPAGNE PRESENTED BY LAURENT PERRIER

SPIRITS COURTESY OF ABSOLUT CITRON

IMPORTED BEER COMPLIMENTS OF HEINEKEN USA

FINE ALES AND LAGERS COMPLIMENTS OF
PYRAMID BREWERIES

WATER COMPLIMENTS OF EVIAN NATURAL SPRING WATER
AND FERRARELLE NATURALLY SPARKLING WATER

GOVERNORS BALL COORDINATION
BY CHERYL CECCHETTO, SEQUOIA PRODUCTIONS

\*\*\*

*GOVERNORS BALL COMMITTEE*
SID GANIS, *Chair*
ALAN BERGMAN, *Vice Chair*

\*\*\*

"Oscar" statuette © AMPAS ®

## ACKNOWLEDGEMENTS TO ALL INVOLVED IN MAKING THIS A FIVE STAR EVENT

**THE BACK PAGE OF THE PROGRAM WITH THE SHRINE
AUDITORIUM SYMBOL**

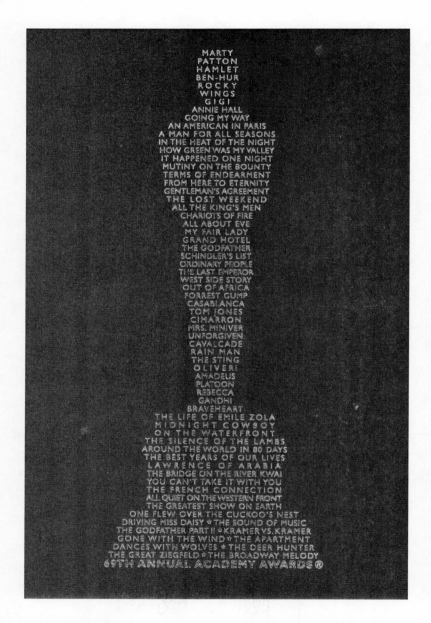

**MY 69th ANNUAL ACADEMY AWARDS SHOW PROGRAM**

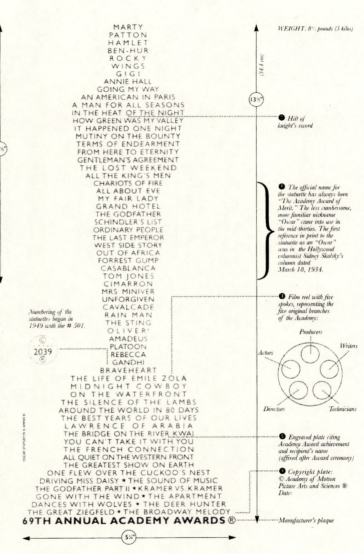

❶ *OSCAR'S birth took place at a Hollywood banquet on May 11, 1927, one week after the Academy of Motion Picture Arts and Sciences was organized. At that meeting, Louis B. Mayer, President of Metro-Goldwyn-Mayer Studios, urged that the Academy create a special film award. Cedric Gibbons, an art director for MGM, was asked to oversee the production of an appropriate prize and symbol for the new Academy. Gibbons approached a young sculptor, George Stanley, and they arrived at a design of a knight holding a crusader's sword* ❷ *standing atop a reel of film,* ❸ *whose five spokes signified the five original branches of the Academy.*

*Stanley's rendering of the statuette was first cast in 1928 by the California Bronze Foundry.*

*From 1928 to 1930, the statuette was hand-cast in bronze with 24 karat gold plating. From 1930 to the present, it has been cast in Britannia metal (an alloy of tin, copper and antimony, very much like hard pewter), then copper-, nickel-, silver- and 24-karat gold-plated, with each application highly polished before the next one is applied.*

❹ *From 1928 to 1945, the base (originally designed by Frederic Hope, assistant to Cedric Gibbons), was Belgian black marble. From 1945 to the present, this base has been made of metal.*

❺ *The design of the statuette was copyrighted by the Academy on September 2, 1941. It has not changed from its original conception, but the size of the base varied until the present standard was adopted for the 1945 (18th) Academy Awards.*

*During World War II, from the 15th presentation in 1942, through the 17th in 1944, plaster statuettes were given. These were replaced with metal ones when the materials became available again after the war.*

*Numbering of the statuettes began in 1949 with the # 501.*

2039

OSCAR STATUETTE © AMPAS

MARTY
PATTON
HAMLET
BEN-HUR
ROCKY
WINGS
GIGI
ANNIE HALL
GOING MY WAY
AN AMERICAN IN PARIS
A MAN FOR ALL SEASONS
IN THE HEAT OF THE NIGHT
HOW GREEN WAS MY VALLEY
IT HAPPENED ONE NIGHT
MUTINY ON THE BOUNTY
TERMS OF ENDEARMENT
FROM HERE TO ETERNITY
GENTLEMAN'S AGREEMENT
THE LOST WEEKEND
ALL THE KING'S MEN
CHARIOTS OF FIRE
ALL ABOUT EVE
MY FAIR LADY
GRAND HOTEL
THE GODFATHER
SCHINDLER'S LIST
ORDINARY PEOPLE
THE LAST EMPEROR
WEST SIDE STORY
OUT OF AFRICA
FORREST GUMP
CASABLANCA
TOM JONES
CIMARRON
MRS MINIVER
UNFORGIVEN
CAVALCADE
RAIN MAN
THE STING
OLIVER!
AMADEUS
PLATOON
REBECCA
GANDHI
BRAVEHEART
THE LIFE OF EMILE ZOLA
MIDNIGHT COWBOY
ON THE WATERFRONT
THE SILENCE OF THE LAMBS
AROUND THE WORLD IN 80 DAYS
THE BEST YEARS OF OUR LIVES
LAWRENCE OF ARABIA
THE BRIDGE ON THE RIVER KWAI
YOU CAN'T TAKE IT WITH YOU
THE FRENCH CONNECTION
ALL QUIET ON THE WESTERN FRONT
THE GREATEST SHOW ON EARTH
ONE FLEW OVER THE CUCKOO'S NEST
DRIVING MISS DAISY ★ THE SOUND OF MUSIC
THE GODFATHER PART II ★ KRAMER VS. KRAMER
GONE WITH THE WIND ★ THE APARTMENT
DANCES WITH WOLVES ★ THE DEER HUNTER
THE GREAT ZIEGFELD ★ THE BROADWAY MELODY

## 69TH ANNUAL ACADEMY AWARDS ®

*WEIGHT: 8½ pounds (3 kilos)*

(34.4 cm)

13½"

❷ *Hilt of knight's sword*

10½"

5¼"

❶ *The official name for the statuette has always been "The Academy Award of Merit." The less cumbersome, more familiar nickname "Oscar" came into use in the mid-thirties. The first reference in print to the statuette as an "Oscar" was in the Hollywood columnist Sidney Skolsky's column dated March 18, 1934.*

❸ *Film reel with five spokes, representing the five original branches of the Academy:*

Producers

Writers

Actors

Directors

Technicians

❻ *Engraved plate citing Academy Award achievement and recipient's name (affixed after Award ceremony)*

❼ *Copyright plate:*
© *Academy of Motion Picture Arts and Sciences* ®
*Date:*

Manufacturer's plaque

# SOME KNOWN FACTS ABOUT MR. OSCAR

OSCAR®

*MONDAY, MARCH 24, 1997*

**MY 69th ANNUAL ACADEMY AWARDS SHOW PROGRAM FROM MARCH 24, 1997**

*You're sitting in a slowly darkening room with several hundred strangers. Conversation ceases, and the atmosphere is charged with expectation and (unless you're at the Academy's theater) popcorn. You're at the movies.*

*We've been gathering in groups to see movies for just over a century now, and the continuing popularity of the experience—and its place in our emotional lives—suggests that something profoundly important happens when we come together to see and hear even the least solemn of motion pictures.*

*The fact that we experience movies communally is a powerful part of their appeal. We're each interacting individually with what is on the screen, but the "groupness" of moviegoing adds immeasurably to its impact.*

*Funny movies are funnier, scary ones scarier in a theater filled with people. Sad moments are more affecting and exhilarating ones take us higher when we share them with a roomful of humanity.*

*So many of the media we interact with today, we experience in isolation: books, our car radios, our computer screens, even television. They all have considerable strengths and virtues, but in a world in which separation and alienation are the order of the day it is satisfying to celebrate a popular art form that encourages togetherness.*

*"Togetherness" not just in a trivial sense, but in a more reflective, we're-all-in-this-life-together-and-we're-going-to-have-to-make-some-decisions sense. Ours is an art form that this past year provoked, in addition to the few hundred conversations that followed almost any individual screening, a national dialogue on issues including relations between races, the limits of free speech, and whether we ought to consider fireproofing the White House and midtown Manhattan.*

*In restricting its province to theatrical films, the Academy of Motion Picture Arts and Sciences has always celebrated an art form that brings us together both physically, as part of an individual audience, and emotionally as part of a national or even a global audience. Tonight, for the 69th time, we celebrate going to the movies . . . together.*

**GIL CATES**
*Producer*

## *ACADEMY OF MOTION PICTURE ARTS AND SCIENCES*

### *OFFICERS*

**ARTHUR HILLER**
*President*

| SID GANIS | ARTHUR HAMILTON | FAY KANIN |
|---|---|---|
| *First Vice President* | *Vice President* | *Vice President* |

ROBERT REHME      RODDY McDOWALL
*Treasurer*         *Secretary*

BRUCE DAVIS
*Executive Director*

### *BOARD OF GOVERNORS*

| | |
|---|---|
| DEDE ALLEN | KATHLEEN KENNEDY |
| JOHN BAILEY | HOWARD W. KOCH |
| CURT R. BEHLMER | MARVIN LEVY |
| CARL BELL | WILLIAM C. LITTLEJOHN |
| CHARLES BERNSTEIN | CAROL LITTLETON |
| ROBERT F. BOYLE | KARL MALDEN |
| BRUCE BROUGHTON | MARVIN MARCH |
| ALLEN DAVIAU | ROGER L. MAYER |
| LINWOOD G. DUNN | RODDY McDOWALL |
| RICHARD EDLUND | DONALD O. MITCHELL |
| JUNE FORAY G | REGORY PECK |
| JOHN FRANKENHEIMER | DANIEL PETRIE, JR. |
| SID GANIS | ROBERT REHME |
| DON HALL | BILL TAYLOR |
| ARTHUR HAMILTON | FRANK J. URIOSTE |
| ARTHUR HILLER | LEW R. WASSERMAN |
| CHERYL BOONE ISAACS | HASKELL WEXLER |
| NORMAN JEWISON | ALBERT WOLSKY |
| FAY KANIN | RICHARD D. ZANUCK |
| HAL KANTER | |

## 69TH ANNUAL ACADEMY AWARDS PRESENTATION

*Producer*
GIL CATES

*Directed by*
LOUIS J. HORVITZ

*Written by*
HAL KANTER
CARRIE FISHER
BUZ KOHAN

*Special Material by*
BILLY CRYSTAL
JOE BOLSTER
ED DRISCOLL
JON MACKS
BILLY MARTIN
MARC SHAIMAN
DAVID STEINBERG
BRUCE VILANCH

*Associate Producer*
MICHAEL B. SELIGMAN

*Executive in Charge of Talent*
DANETTE HERMAN

*Production Designer*
ROY CHRISTOPHER

*Music Director*
BILL CONTI

*Choreographer*
OTIS SALLID

*Lighting Designer*
BOB DICKINSON

*Film Sequences Supervised by*
DOUGLASS M. STEWART, JR.

*Fashion Coordinator*
FRED HAYMAN

*Business Manager*
ROBERT F. METZLER

*PROGRAM*

*AWARDS*

*ACTOR IN A SUPPORTING ROLE*
*ART DIRECTION*
*COSTUME DESIGN*
*SOUND EFFECTS EDITING*
*MAKEUP*
*ACTRESS IN A SUPPORTING ROLE*
*SHORT FILM AWARDS*
*HONORARY AWARD TO MICHAEL KIDD*
*SCIENTIFIC AND TECHNICAL AWARDS*
*DOCUMENTARY AWARDS*
*VISUAL EFFECTS*
*SOUND*
*FILM EDITING*
*ORIGINAL SCORE AWARDS*
*CINEMATOGRAPHY*
*IRVING G. THALBERG AWARD TO SAUL ZAENTZ*
*FOREIGN LANGUAGE FILM*
*ORIGINAL SONG*
*WRITING AWARDS*
*ACTRESS IN A LEADING ROLE*
*ACTOR IN A LEADING ROLE*
*DIRECTOR*
*BEST PICTURE*

\*\*\*

*AN ACADEMY HONORARY AWARD IS PRESENTED*
*TO MICHAEL KIDD IN RECOGNITION OF HIS SERVICES TO*
*THE ART OF THE DANCE IN THE ART OF THE SCREEN*

*THE IRVING G. THALBERG AWARD IS PRESENTED TO SAUL*
*ZAENTZ IN RECOGNITION OF HIS CONSISTENT HIGH*
*QUALITY OF MOTION PICTURE PRODUCTION*

## PRESENTERS

### BILLY CRYSTAL
*Host*

JULIE ANDREWS
ANGELA BASSETT
JULIETTE BINOCHE
BEAVIS & BUTT-HEAD
KENNETH BRANAGH
SANDRA BULLOCK
NICOLAS CAGE
JIM CARREY
GLENN CLOSE
CLAIRE DANES
MICHAEL DOUGLAS
CHRIS FARLEY
JODIE FOSTER
MEL GIBSON
GOLDIE HAWN
SALMA HAYEK
ARTHUR HILLER
GREGORY HINES
HELEN HUNT
TOMMY LEE JONES

DIANE KEATON
NICOLE KIDMAN
COURTNEY LOVE
ANDIE MacDOWELL
STEVE MARTIN
BETTE MIDLER
CHRIS O'DONNELL
AL PACINO
DEBBIE REYNOLDS
TIM ROBBINS
WINONA RYDER
SUSAN SARANDON
KRISTIN SCOTT THOMAS
WILL SMITH
MIRA SORVINO
KEVIN SPACEY
DAVID SPADE
JACK VALENTI
SIGOURNEY WEAVER

FEATURED PERFORMERS
"You Must Love Me"
MADONNA

"For the First Time"
KENNY LOGGINS

"Because You Loved Me"
CELINE DION

"I Finally Found Someone"
NATALIE COLE
ARTURO SANDOVAL

SPECIAL "FILM EDITING"
PERFORMANCE
MICHAEL FLATLEY and LORD
OF THE DANCE

PRODUCTION STAFF
Associate Directors
JIM TANKER
CHRISTINE CLARK BRADLEY
DEBBIE PALACIO
MARILYN SEABURY
SHARON TAYLOR

Production Supervisor
JOHN M. BEST

Script Supervisors
JEFFREY R. RUDEEN
JILL JACKSON

Script Coordinators
JESSE MILLER
JENNIFER MISCHER

Talent Coordinators
CHRISTINE CALANDRA
JULIE KANEKO
SCOTT A. FIFER

Assistant to the Producer
JULIE FAUST

Assistants to the Director
TRACY GROSS
JANIS UHLEY

Assistant to the Associate Producer
CHARLOTTE MINA WEBER

Production Manager
KATHY ERICKSON

Production Coordinators
BILL URBAN
AMY GARDNER
LOIS CASCIO
ALEX DERVIN

Public Relations for the Producer
CHUCK WARN

Production Publicity
NICOLE VON RUDEN

MUSIC
BILL CONTI
BOB BORNSTEIN
JEANNE WOODBURY
NATHAN KAPROFF
SALLY STEVENS
FAE SHEPARD

ORCHESTRATORS
JACK ESKEW
ASHLEY IRWIN
WILLIAM MOTZING
EDDIE KARAM
GORDON GOODWIN
TOM RANIER
BETH ERTZ
MIKE BARONE
CRAIG GARFINKLE

DANCE
Assistant Choreographer
MARIA LEONE

LORD OF THE DANCE
*Dancers*
MICHAEL FLATLEY
BERNADETTE FLYNN
DAIRE NOLAN
GILLIAN NORRIS
DES BAILEY
KELLIE BREEN
STEVEN BRUNNING
DECLAN BUCKE
JOHN CAREY
LINDA CAWTE
DONAL CONLON
KERRIE CONNOLLY
JAMES DEVINE
HELEN EGAN
ATTRACTA FARRELL
DENISE FLYNN
MARK GILLEY
CAROLINE GREEN
EMMETT GRIFFIN
CATRIONA HALE
FIONA HAROLD
KATHLEEN KEADY
MAIREAD KENNEDY
KELLYANN LEATHEM
DEARBHLA LENNON
TONY LUNDON
PATRICK LUNDON
KAREN McCAMPHILL
DEREK MORAN
CHELSEA MULDOON
JIM MURRIHY
ARELEEN Ni BHAOILL
CIAN NOLAN
PAUL NOONAN
SHARON O'BRIEN
DAMIEN O'KANE
COLLEEN ROBERTS
MARY ANN SCHADE-LYNCH
CONOR SMITH
DAWN TIERNAN

THAT THING YOU DO!
*Dancers*
ADRIAN ARMAS
DONIELLE ARTESE
AL BEE
MICHELLE BERUBE
SERGIO CARBAJAL
DOMINIC CARBONE
KELLY COOPER
PALMER DAVIS
JOAQUIN ESCAMILLA
BOB GAYNOR
EDGAR GODINEAUX
STACY HARPER
RYAN HEFFINGTON
JT HORENSTEIN
GEORGE HUBELA
GIGI HUNTER
MELISSA HURLEY
JOHN JACQUET
CRISTAN JUDD
MARIA LEONE
TERRY LINDHOLM
DOMINIC MALDONADO
DIANE MIZOTA
PHINEAS NEWBORN
NANCY O'MEARA
RANDI PAREIRA
MIA PITTS
LIZ RAMOS
TIARAYA SOO
ANGELA STOVER
LISA THOMPSON
CHEKESHA VAN PUTTON

*Featured Performers*
DAVID BACON
STEVE GIRARDI
SHAWN HOFFMAN
JARED KAHN

## *NOMINATIONS*

### *FOR PERFORMANCE BY AN ACTOR IN A SUPPORTING ROLE*
Cuba Gooding, Jr. *in* JERRY MAGUIRE *(TriStar)*

William H. Macy *in* FARGO *(Gramercy)*

Armin Mueller-Stahl *in* SHINE *(Fine Line Features)*

Edward Norton *in* PRIMAL FEAR *(Paramount in Association with Rysher Entertainment)*

James Woods *in* GHOSTS OF MISSISSIPPI *(Columbia)*

### *FOR ACHIEVEMENT IN ART DIRECTION*

THE BIRDCAGE *(MGM/UA)*
*Art Direction:* Bo Welch; *Set Decoration:* Cheryl Carasik

THE ENGLISH PATIENT *(Miramax)*
*Art Direction:* Stuart Craig; *Set Decoration:* Stephenie McMillan

EVITA *(Buena Vista)*
*Art Direction:* Brian Morris; *Set Decoration:* Philippe Turlure

HAMLET *(Columbia) Art Direction:* Tim Harvey

WILLIAM SHAKESPEARE'S ROMEO & JULIET *(20ᵗʰ Century Fox)*
*Art Direction:* Catherine Martin; *Set Decoration:* Brigitte Broch

### *FOR ACHIEVEMENT IN COSTUME DESIGN*

ANGELS AND INSECTS *(Samuel Goldwyn Company)* Paul Brown

EMMA *(Miramax)* Ruth Myers

THE ENGLISH PATIENT *(Miramax)* Ann Roth

HAMLET *(Columbia)* Alex Byrne

THE PORTRAIT OF A LADY *(Gramercy)* Janet Patterson

## *FOR ACHIEVEMENT IN SOUND EFFECTS EDITING*

DAYLIGHT *(Universal)* Richard L. Anderson and David A. Whittaker

ERASER *(Warner Bros.)* Alan Robert Murray and Bub Asman

THE GHOST AND THE DARKNESS *(Paramount)* Bruce Stambler

*Talk about being 'born again.' It's the one time in my life when I had such happiness I couldn't even share it with another human being. I ducked the party, lost the crowds and took a walk. Just me and Oscar. I think I relived my entire lifetime that night as I walked up and down the streets of Beverly Hills.*

Frank Sinatra
Special Award, 1945
Best Supporting Actor, 1953
Hersholt Award, 1970

## *FOR ACHIEVEMENT IN MAKEUP*

GHOSTS OF MISSISSIPPI *(Columbia)*
MATTHEW W. MUNGLE and DEBORAH LA MIA DENAVER

THE NUTTY PROFESSOR *(Universal)* RICK BAKER and DAVID LEROY ANDERSON

STAR TREK: FIRST CONTACT *(Paramount)*
MICHAEL WESTMORE, SCOTT WHEELER and JAKE GARBER

## *FOR PERFORMANCE BY AN ACTRESS IN A SUPPORTING ROLE*

JOAN ALLEN *in* THE CRUCIBLE *(20th Century Fox)*

LAUREN BACALL *in* THE MIRROR HAS TWO FACES *(TriStar)*

JULIETTE BINOCHE *in* THE ENGLISH PATIENT *(Miramax)*

BARBARA HERSHEY *in* THE PORTRAIT OF A LADY *(Gramercy)*

MARIANNE JEAN-BAPTISTE *in* SECRETS & LIES *(October Films)*

## *FOR BEST ANIMATED SHORT FILM*

CANHEAD *A Timothy Hittle Production*, TIMOTHY HITTLE and CHRIS PETERSON

LA SALLA *A National Film Board of Canada Production*, RICHARD CONDIE

QUEST *A Thomas Stellmach Animation Production*,
TYRON MONTGOMERY and THOMAS STELLMACH

WAT'S PIG *An Aardman Animations Limited Production*, PETER LORD

## *FOR BEST LIVE ACTION SHORT FILM*

DE TRIPAS, CORAZÓN *An IMCINE/DPC/Universidad de Guadalajara Production,*
ANTONIO URRUTIA

DEAR DIARY *A Dream Works SKG Production*, David Frankel and Barry Jossen
ERNST & LYSET *An M & M Production*,
Kim Magnusson and Anders Thomas Jensen

ESPOSADOS *A Zodiac Films/Juan Carlos Fresnadillo P.C. Production*,
Juan Carlos Fresnadillo

WORDLESS *A Film Trust Italia Production*,
Bernadette Carranza and Antonello De Leo

## *FOR BEST DOCUMENTARY SHORT SUBJECT*

BREATHING LESSONS: THE LIFE AND WORK OF MARK O'BRIEN
*An Inscrutable Films/Pacific News Service Production*, JESSICA YU

COSMIC VOYAGE *A Cosmic Voyage Inc. Production*,
JEFFREY MARVIN and BAYLEY SILLECK

AN ESSAY ON MATISSE
*A Great Projects Film Company, Inc. Production*, PERRY WOLFF

SPECIAL EFFECTS *A NOVA/WGBH Boston Production*,
SUSANNE SIMPSON and BEN BURTT

*THE WILD BUNCH:* AN ALBUM IN MONTAGE
*A Tyrus Entertainment Production*, PAUL SEYDOR and NICK REDMAN

## *FOR BEST DOCUMENTARY FEATURE*

THE LINE KING: THE AL HIRSCHFELD STORY
*A New York Times History Production*, SUSAN W. DRYFOOS

MANDELA *(Island Pictures) A Clinica Estetico, Ltd. Production*,
JO MENELL and ANGUS GIBSON

SUZANNE FARRELL: ELUSIVE MUSE *A Seahorse Films, Inc. Production*,
ANNE BELLE and DEBORAH DICKSON

TELL THE TRUTH AND RUN: GEORGE SELDES AND THE
AMERICAN PRESS
*A Never Tire Production*, RICK GOLDSMITH

WHEN WE WERE KINGS *(Gramercy) A DASFilms Ltd. Production*,
LEON GAST and DAVID SONENBERG

## *FOR ACHIEVEMENT IN VISUAL EFFECTS*

DRAGONHEART *(Universal)*
Scott Squires, Phil Tippett, James Straus and Kit West

INDEPENDENCE DAY *(20th Century Fox)*
Volker Engel, Douglas Smith, Clay Pinney and Joseph Viskocil

TWISTER *(Warner Bros. and Universal)*
Stefen Fangmeier, John Frazier, Habib Zargarpour and Henry La Bounta

*Even in Europe the Oscar is recognized as the highest award a filmmaker can receive. It is just as highly-coveted in Italy as it is here.*
Carlo Rambaldi
Visual Effects, 1976; 1979; 1982

## *FOR BEST DOCUMENTARY SHORT SUBJECT*

BREATHING LESSONS: THE LIFE AND WORK OF MARK O'BRIEN
*An Inscrutable Films/Pacific News Service Production*, Jessica Yu

COSMIC VOYAGE *A Cosmic Voyage Inc. Production*,
Jeffrey Marvin and Bayley Silleck

AN ESSAY ON MATISSE
*A Great Projects Film Company, Inc. Production*, Perry Wolff

SPECIAL EFFECTS *A NOVA/WGBH Boston Production*,
Susanne Simpson and Ben Burtt

*THE WILD BUNCH:* AN ALBUM IN MONTAGE
*A Tyrus Entertainment Production*, Paul Seydor and Nick Redman

## *FOR BEST DOCUMENTARY FEATURE*

THE LINE KING: THE AL HIRSCHFELD STORY
*A New York Times History Production*, Susan W. Dryfoos

MANDELA *(Island Pictures) A Clinica Estetico, Ltd. Production*,
Jo Menell and Angus Gibson

SUZANNE FARRELL: ELUSIVE MUSE *A Seahorse Films, Inc. Production*,
Anne Belle and Deborah Dickson

TELL THE TRUTH AND RUN: GEORGE SELDES AND THE
AMERICAN PRESS
*A Never Tire Production*, Rick Goldsmith

WHEN WE WERE KINGS *(Gramercy) A DASFilms Ltd. Production*,
Leon Gast and David Sonenberg

## *FOR ACHIEVEMENT IN VISUAL EFFECTS*

DRAGONHEART *(Universal)*
Scott Squires, Phil Tippett, James Straus and Kit West

INDEPENDENCE DAY *(20th Century Fox)*
Volker Engel, Douglas Smith, Clay Pinney and Joseph Viskocil

TWISTER *(Warner Bros. and Universal)*
Stefen Fangmeier, John Frazier, Habib Zargarpour and Henry La Bounta

*Even in Europe the Oscar is recognized as the highest award a filmmaker can receive. It is just as highly-coveted in Italy as it is here.*
Carlo Rambaldi
Visual Effects, 1976; 1979; 1982

## *FOR ACHIEVEMENT IN SOUND*

THE ENGLISH PATIENT *(Miramax)* WALTER MURCH,
MARK BERGER, DAVID PARKER and CHRIS NEWMAN

EVITA *(Buena Vista)* ANDY NELSON, ANNA BEHLMER and KEN WESTON

INDEPENDENCE DAY *(20th Century Fox)* CHRIS CARPENTER,
BILL W. BENTON, BOB BEEMER and JEFF WEXLER

THE ROCK *(Buena Vista)* KEVIN O'CONNELL,
GREG P. RUSSELL and KEITH A. WESTER

TWISTER *(Warner Bros. and Universal)* STEVE MASLOW, GREGG LANDAKER,
KEVIN O'CONNELL and GEOFFREY PATTERSON

## *FOR ACHIEVEMENT IN FILM EDITING*

*THE ENGLISH PATIENT (Miramax)* WALTER MURCH

EVITA *(Buena Vista)* GERRY HAMBLING

FARGO *(Gramercy)* RODERICK JAYNES

JERRY MAGUIRE *(TriStar)* JOE HUTSHING

SHINE *(Fine Line Features)* PIP KARMEL

## *FOR ACHIEVEMENT IN MUSIC*
## *(ORIGINAL MUSICAL OR COMEDY SCORE)*

EMMA *(Miramax)* RACHEL PORTMAN

THE FIRST WIVES CLUB *(Paramount)* MARC SHAIMAN

THE HUNCHBACK OF NOTRE DAME *(Buena Vista)*
*Music by* ALAN MENKEN, *Lyrics by* STEPHEN SCHWARTZ,
*Orchestral Score by* ALAN MENKEN

JAMES AND THE GIANT PEACH *(Buena Vista)* RANDY NEWMAN

THE PREACHER'S WIFE *(Buena Vista)* HANS ZIMMER

## *FOR ACHIEVEMENT IN MUSIC (ORIGINAL DRAMATIC SCORE)*

THE ENGLISH PATIENT *(Miramax)* GABRIEL YARED

HAMLET *(Columbia)* PATRICK DOYLE

MICHAEL COLLINS *(Geffen Pictures through Warner Bros.)* ELLIOT GOLDENTHAL

SHINE *(Fine Line Features)* DAVID HIRSCHFELDER

SLEEPERS *(Warner Bros.)* JOhn WILLIAMS

## *FOR ACHIEVEMENT IN CINEMATOGRAPHY*

THE ENGLISH PATIENT *(Miramax)* JOHN SEALE

EVITA *(Buena Vista)* DARIUS KHONDJI

FARGO *(Gramercy)* ROGER DEAKINS

FLY AWAY HOME *(Columbia)* CALEB DESCHANEL

MICHAEL COLLINS *(Geffen Pictures through Warner Bros.)* CHRIS MENGES

## *BEST FOREIGN LANGUAGE FILM*

A CHEF IN LOVE *An Adam and Even Production* (GEORGIA)

KOLYA *A Biograf Jan Sverac / Portobello Pictures / Ceska Televize / Pandora Cinema Production* (CZECH REPUBLIC)

THE OTHER SIDE OF SUNDAY *An NRK Dram Production* (NORWAY)

PRISONER OF THE MOUNTAINS *A Caravan JSC / B.G. Production* (RUSSIA)

RIDICULE *An Epithete / Cinea Production* (FRANCE)

*I would like to take my space here to thank the Academy for two marvelous nights shared with my Huckleberry friend Johnny Mercer.*
HENRY MANCINI
Music (Scoring of Dramatic or Comedy Picture), 1961
Music (Song), 1961; 1962
Music (Song Score and Adaptation Score), 1982

## *FOR ACHIEVEMENT IN MUSIC (ORIGINAL SONG)*

"Because You Loved Me" *from* UP CLOSE AND PERSONAL *(Buena Vista)*
*Music and Lyric by* Diane Warren

"For the First Time" *from* ONE FINE DAY *(20th Century Fox)*
*Music and Lyric by* James Newton Howard,
Jud J. Friedman and Allan Dennis Rich

"I Finally Found Someone" *from* THE MIRROR HAS TWO FACES *(TriStar)*
*Music and Lyric by* Barbra Streisand, Marvin Hamlisch,
Bryan Adams and Robert "Mutt" Lange

"That Thing You Do!" *from* THAT THING YOU DO! *(20th Century Fox)*
*Music and Lyric by* Adam Schlesinger

"You Must Love Me" *from* EVITA *(Buena Vista)*
*Music by* Andrew Lloyd Webber, *Lyric by* Tim Rice

## *FOR SCREENPLAY WRITTEN DIRECTLY FOR THE SCREEN*

FARGO *(Gramercy) Written by* Ethan Coen & Joel Coen

JERRY MAGUIRE *(TriStar) Written by* Cameron Crowe

LONE STAR *(Sony Pictures Classics) Written by* John Sayles

SECRETS & LIES *(October Films) Written by* Mike Leigh

SHINE *(Fine Line Features) Screenplay by* Jan Sardi; *Story by* Scott Hicks

## *FOR SCREENPLAY BASED ON MATERIAL*
## *PREVIOUSLY PRODUCED OR PUBLISHED*

THE CRUCIBLE *(20th Century Fox) Screenplay by* Arthur Miller

THE ENGLISH PATIENT *(Miramax) Screenplay by* Anthony Minghella

HAMLET *(Columbia) Adapted for the screen by* Kenneth Branagh

SLING BLADE *(Miramax) Written by* Billy Bob Thornton

TRAINSPOTTING *(Miramax) Screenplay by* John Hodge

# *FOR PERFORMANCE BY AN ACTRESS IN A LEADING ROLE*

BRENDA BLETHYN *in* SECRETS & LIES *(October Films)*

DIANE KEATON *in* MARVIN'S ROOM *(Miramax)*

FRANCES McDORMAND *in* FARGO *(Gramercy)*

KRISTIN SCOTT THOMAS *in* THE ENGLISH PATIENT *(Miramax)*

EMILY WATSON *in* BREAKING THE WAVES *(October Films)*

# *FOR PERFORMANCE BY AN ACTOR IN A LEADING ROLE*

TOM CRUISE *in* JERRY MAGUIRE *(TriStar)*

RALPH FIENNES *in* THE ENGLISH PATIENT *(Miramax)*

WOODY HARRELSON *in* THE PEOPLE vs. LARRY FLYNT *(Columbia)*

GEOFFREY RUSH *in* SHINE *(Fine Line Features)*

BILLY BOB THORNTON *in* SLING BLADE *(Miramax)*

# *FOR ACHIEVEMENT IN DIRECTING*

THE ENGLISH PATIENT *(Miramax)* ANTHONY MINGHELLA

FARGO *(Gramercy)* JOEL COEN

THE PEOPLE vs. LARRY FLYNT *(Columbia)* MILOS FORMAN

SECRETS & LIES *(October Films)* MIKE LEIGH

SHINE *(Fine Line Features)* SCOTT HICKS

## *FOR BEST PICTURE*

THE ENGLISH PATIENT *(Miramax) A Tiger Moth Production*
Saul Zaentz, *Producer*
FARGO *(Gramercy) A Working Title Production* Ethan Coen, *Producer*

JERRY MAGUIRE *(TriStar) A TriStar Pictures Production*
James L. Brooks, Laurence Mark, Richard Sakai
And Cameron Crowe, *Producers*

SECRETS & LIES *(October Films) A Ciby 2000 and Thin Man Films Production*
Simon Channing-Williams, *Producer*

SHINE *(Fine Line Features) A Momentum Films Production* Jane Scott,
*Producer*

*My thoughts for a special award for* HENRY V *in 1947 and for* HAMLET *in '48 for performance and best picture were for each and both of the most delighted kind and my gratitude of the heartfelt fullest.*

Laurence Olivier
Special Award, 1946
Best Actor, 1948
Honorary Award, 1978

## *TECHNICAL ACHIEVEMENT AWARDS (CERTIFICATES)*

To Perry Kivolowitz, for the primary design, and Dr. Garth A. Dickie for the development of the algorithms for the shape-driven warping and morphing subsystem of the Elastic Reality Special Effects System.
*These components form the core of an efficient and easy-to-use system which greatly simplifies the creation of shape-changing visual effects in motion pictures.*

To Ken Perlin for the development of Perlin Noise, a technique used to produce natural appearing textures on computer generated surfaces for motion picture visual effects.
*The development of Perlin Noise has allowed computer graphics artists to better represent the complexity of natural phenomena in visual effects for the motion picture industry.*

To Nestor Burtnyk and Marceli Wein of the National Research Council of Canada for their pioneering work in the development of software techniques for Computer Assisted Key Framing for Character Animation.
*The pioneering work of Mr. Burtnyk and Dr. Wein demonstrated the first significant use of the computer in two dimensional key-frame character animation and influenced many subsequent developments in computer animation techniques.*

To Grant Loucks for the concept and specifications of the Mark V Director's Viewfinder.

*The Mark V has simplified the operation and extended the range of a valuable tool used for previewing scenes covering a wide range of lens focal lenths and film formats.*

To Brian Knep, Craig Hayes, Rick Sayre and Thomas Williams for the creation and development of the Direct Input Device.

*The Direct Input Device is an encoded armature which allows stop-motion animators to bring their skills and artistry directly into computer animation.*

To James Kajiya and Timothy Kay for their pioneering work in producing computer generated fur and hair in motion pictures.

*This pioneering work inspired the development of the computer-generated fur and hair systems that are in use today.*

To Jeffrey Yost, Christian Rouet, David Benson and Florian Kainz for the development of a system to create and control computer generated fur and hair in motion pictures.

*This system represents a significant advancement for controlling computer generated short fur and long hair in a motion picture production environment.*

To Richard A. Prey and William N. Masten for the design and development of the Nite Sun II lighting crane and camera platform.

*The Nite Sun II is a mobile crane system for location lighting and camera use. This unique, self-contained system with its platform, has the ability to lift 1200 lbs. of personnel, lighting and camera equipment up to 124 feet above the ground.*

## *SCIENTIFIC AND ENGINEERING AWARDS (PLAQUES)*

TO JOHN SCHLAG, BRIAN KNEP, ZORAN KAČIĆ-ALESIĆ AND THOMAS WILLIAMS FOR THE DEVELOPMENT OF THE VIEWPAINT 3D PAINT SYSTEM FOR FILM PRODUCTION WORK.
*ViewPaint is an interactive 3D paint system that allows artists to apply color and texture details to computer generated effects.*


TO WILLIAM REEVES FOR THE ORIGINAL CONCEPT AND THE DEVELOPMENT OF PARTICLE SYSTEMS USED TO CREATE COMPUTER GENERATED VISUAL EFFECTS IN MOTION PICTURES.
*The concept of particle systems inspired and continues to influence further developments in the area of computer generated tornadoes, flames, sparks, snow, clouds and other visual effects.*


TO JIM HOURIHAN FOR THE PRIMARY DESIGN AND DEVELOPMENT OF THE INTERACTIVE LANGUAGE-BASED CONTROL OF PARTICLE SYSTEMS AS EMBODIED IN THE DYNAMATION SOFTWARE PACKAGE.
*Dynamation is used to create a wide variety of computer generated effects such as tornadoes, flames, sparks, snow and clouds in motion pictures.*

TO JONATHAN ERLAND AND KAY BEVING ERLAND FOR THE DEVELOPMENT OF THE DIGITAL SERIES TRAVELING MATTE BACKING SYSTEM USED FOR COMPOSITE PHOTOGRAPHY IN MOTION PICTURES.
*This system reduces both the time and expense of shooting and posting composite photography.*
*The spectral reflectance of the backing material, paint formulation, and the spectral transmission of the flourescent lamps match the peak sensitivity of the recommended camera film.*

## *ACADEMY AWARD OF MERIT (OSCAR)*

(Originally awarded a Scientific and Engineering Award [plaque] in 1985, this is an "upgrade" award.)

To Imax Corporation for the method of filming and exhibiting high-fidelity, large-format, wide-angle motion pictures.

*Integral to the process for presenting cinema programs in the IMAX or IMAX Dome format is the rolling loop projector, developed from a film transport mechanism originally invented by P.R.W. Jones. Improvements made on the patent by the IMAX Corporation, and the development of other peripheral equipment, made possible the high-speed, horizontal projection of 70mm pictures, fifteen perforations per frame, onto screens of unusually large proportions in theaters designed to specifications for optimum viewing of those motion pictures. An exceptional sense of participation is experienced by audiences when pictures, photographed to the requirements of the process, are shown in IMAX or IMAX Dome theaters.*


## *AWARD OF COMMENDATION (SPECIAL PLAQUE)*

(Awarded to acknowledge special technical contributions to the motion picture industry.)

Joe Lombardi

*In celebration of fifty years in the motion picture industry. His knowledge and leadership in the field of pyrotechnics and special effects along with his uncompromising promotion of safety on the set have established the standard for today's special effects technicians.*


## *JOHN A. BONNER MEDAL OF COMMENDATION (MEDALLION)*

(Awarded in appreciation for outstanding service and dedication in upholding the high standards of the Academy of Motion Picture Arts and Sciences.)

Volker W. Bahnemann

Burton "Bud" Stone

## *SCIENTIFIC AND TECHNICAL AWARDS COMMITTEE*

EDMUND M. DiGIULIO, *Chair*
RICHARD EDLUND, *Vice Chair*
CURT R. BEHLMER
BOB BURTON
ED CATMULL
DENNY CLAIRMONT
FRANK (PETE) CLARK
CLAY DAVIS
EDWARD EFRON
JONATHAN ERLAND
RAY FEENEY
DOUGLAS FRIES
RICHARD B. GLICKMAN
DAVID W. GRAY
DON HALL
RICHARD HOLLANDER
GEORGE T. HOWARD
DAVID INGLISH
DON IWERKS
VICTOR KEMPER
MARK KIMBALL

JOEL F. KIRSCHNER
TOM KUHN
HOWARD T. LaZARE
TAD MARBURG
MIKE MICHELSON
TAKUO MIYAGISHIMA
COLIN MOSSMAN
BOB NETTMANN
BEVERLY PASTERCZYK
J. KEVIN PIKE
BOB PINKSTON
ROBERT PRIMES
DONALD C. ROGERS
RODERICK T. RYAN
JUERGEN SCHWINZER
ARNOLD SHUPACK
RICHARD J. STUMPF
BILL TAYLOR
GREG THAGARD
PAUL VLAHOS

## AWARDS RULES COMMITTEE

ALLEN DAVIAU, *Chair*
ROBERT REHME, *Vice Chair*
CARL BELL
ROBERT F. BOYLE
MARTHA COOLIDGE
RICHARD EDLUND
DON HALL
ARTHUR HAMILTON
CHERYL BOONE ISAACS
HAL KANTER
RODDY McDOWALL
ARTHUR SCHMIDT
RICHARD D. ZANUCK

## PUBLIC RELATIONS COORDINATING COMMITTEE

MARVIN LEVY, *Chair*
SID GANIS, *Vice Chair*
NADIA ALVES-BRONSON
HOLLACE DAVIDS
SID GANIS
BETHLYN HAND
CHERYL BOONE ISAACS
ARLENE LUDWIG
JULIAN MYERS
DALE C. OLSON
JERRY PAM
JUDITH SCHWAM
DANIEL WHEATCROFT

## GOVERNORS BALL COMMITTEE

SID GANIS, *Chair*
ALAN BERGMAN, *Vice Chair*

## FOREIGN LANGUAGE FILM AWARD EXECUTIVE COMMITTEE

FAY KANIN, *Chair*
NINA FOCH, *Vice Chair*
GENE ALLEN
ASHOK AMRITRAJ
FRANK CAPRA, JR.
RAFFAELLA DE LAURENTIIS
CALEB DESCHANEL
RUDI A. FEHR
JUNE FORAY
MICHAEL GOLDMAN
REGINA GRUSS
DOLORES RUBIN LEVIN
DAMIAN LONDON
LISA LU
SVEN NYKVIST
JONAS ROSENFIELD, JR.
GEORGE SCHAEFER
ROBERT E. WISE

## DOCUMENTARY AWARDS EXECUTIVE COMMITTEE

WALTER SHENSON, *Chair*
CHARLES BERNSTEIN, *Vice Chair*
DIMITRA ARLYS
BERT F. BALSAM
JEAN ROUVEROL BUTLER
MARK J. HARRIS
JAMES C. KATZ
DAMIAN LONDON
FREIDA LEE MOCK
TERRY SANDERS
S. DAVID SAXON
ARNOLD SCHWARTZMAN
CHUCK WORKMAN
PETER ZINNER

**1996 FILM SEQUENCE AND FILM EDITING MONTAGE**

*By* CHUCK WORKMAN

*Associate Producer*
JENNIFER McGONIGAL

*Assistant Editor*
H. SCOTT RANDOL

*Production Assistant*
BRIAN RADLINSKI

**SHAKESPEARE SEQUENCE AND MEMORIAL TRIBUTE**

*By* MICHAEL J. SHAPIRO

*Editor*
TERRY STOKES

*Associate Producer*
SCOTT McISAAC

*Production Coordinator*
DIRK MEENAN

**SAUL ZAENTZ TRIBUTE AND "GOING TO THE MOVIES"**

*By* JON BLOOM

*Producer*
RICHARD REDFIELD

*Editor*
KORT FALKENBERG III

*Researchers*
LYNN PECK, KIM LIMTIACO, ALEXANDRA DOHERTY

*Finishing*
DARREN PURCELL

**MICHAEL KIDD TRIBUTE**

*By* SHANDA SAWYER

*Editor*
ROSS GUIDICI

*Assistant*
GABRIELLA ZIELINSKI

**"BILLY'S" FILM**

*By* TROY MILLER

*Producer*
TOM SHERREN

*Director of Photography*
CLYDE SMITH

*Art Director*
DAN BUTTS

*Editor*
STEVEN WELCH

*Production Supervisor*
GAIL SMERIGAN

*Post Production Supervisor*
FRANK C. AGNONE II

*Film Coordinator*
HEATHER VINCENT

*Editors*
ROBERT MALACHOWSKI, JR.
KEVIN PROULX

*Production Assistants*
TERRILL BAZILE
JAMES COOPER
BRIAN DIETCH
XANDRO DONADO
ANNETTE FULLER

BRIAN HALL
MITCH HARRINGTON
TOM HOGAN
STEVE ICHIHO
VANESSA McCARTHY
TANYA MICHNEVICH
JOHN MUSSMAN
SANDY PIERCE
SERGE ROCCO
GERARD ROJO
ERIC SCHRIER
ANDREA WAGNER-BARTON

## *ACKNOWLEDGEMENTS*

To the Documentary Awards Committee, the Foreign Language Film Award Committee, the Makeup Award Rules Committee, the Short Film Awards Committee, the Sound Effects Editing Award Rules Committee, and the Visual Effects Award Rules Committee for diligent and conscientious performance of their duties throughout the year.

The Academy wishes to thank the following for granting it permission to include clips from various motion pictures in the 69th Annual Academy Awards presentation:
Mr. Woody Allen, Amblin Entertainment, Inc., Aries, Estate of Louis J. Armstrong, Mr. Marlon Brando, British Film Institute, Canadian Broadcasting Corporation, Canal+Distribution, Mr. Jim Carrey, Castle Hill Productions, Castle Rock Entertainment, Cinepix Film Properties, Inc., Columbia Pictures, Comedy III Productions, Mr. Tom Cruise, Ms. Geena Davis, Dimension Films, Disney Enterprises, Inc., Filmopolis Pictures, Fine Line Features, General Cinema Theaters, Mr. Mel Gibson, Gramercy Pictures, Hollywood Pictures, Image Bank, ITC Entertainment Group, Mr. Michael Kidd, Ms. Shelah Hackett Kidd, King Features, Kinnevic Media Properties, Kultar Video, Madonna, The Mary Pickford Company, MCA/Universal, Merchant Ivory Productions, Metro-Goldwyn-Mayer Inc., Miramax Films, Morgan Creek Productions, New Line Cinema Corporation, New World Video, Mr. Jack Nicholson, October Films, Orion Classics, a Division of Metromedia Entertainment Group, Paramount Pictures, Polygram, Rank Film Distributors Limited, Rastar Productions, Republic Entertainment Inc., The Rodgers and Hammerstein Organization, Ms. Meg Ryan, Rysher Entertainment, The Samuel Goldwyn Company, The Saul Zaentz Company, Mr. Arnold Schwarzenegger, Sony Pictures Classics, Mr. Sylvester Stallone, Mr. Ray Stark, The Estate of John Steinbeck, Mr. Phil Stern, Ms. Barbra Streisand, Mr. John Travolta, Tristar Pictures, Turner Entertainment, TV Matters, Twentieth Century Fox Film Corporation, Warner Bros., Mr. Denzel Washington, The Estate of Orson Welles, Mr. Robin Williams, Mr. Robert Wise, WNET.

To the Screen Actors Guild, the Directors Guild of America, the Writers Guild of America, the American Federation of Musicians, the American Federation of Television and Radio Artists, the Motion Picture Association of America, Actors Equity, Theatre Authority, Inc., and the American Motion Picture Exhibitors for their cooperation.

To Robert Iger, David Westin, Jamie Tarses, John Hamlin, Alan Sternfeld, Marilyn Wilson, Tom Van Schaick, Preston Davis, and Robert L. Young of ABC Inc., and to the production staff of ABC: Jim Kussman, John M. McElveney, Sue Arrington, Joe Neary, Tony Neely, Stan Weber, Nancy Kohatsu, Arturo Gonzalez, Doug Dessero, Burt Schwartz, and Dave Morris, whose cooperation and assistance are so valuable to the success of the Academy Awards Presentation.

To the Armed Forces Radio and Television Service and Air Force Colonel Glen L. Brady for carrying the television broadcast and filmed record of the Awards Presentation to our Armed Forces around the world.

To Mayor Richard J. Riordan's office, Chief Willie Williams and the Los Angeles Police Department, the California Highway Patrol and the Los Angeles Department of Transportation for coordinating traffic control for this event. To Chief Engineer William R. Bamattre and the Los Angeles Fire Department for coordinating public safety and fire protection facilities.

To Jerry Moon and Pinkerton for planning and executing security arrangements for this event.

Billy Crystal's tuxedo designed by Giorgio Armani.

The following designers have furnished fashions for nominees and presenters for the Academy Awards:

Alberto Ferretti, Angel Sanchez, Anna Sui, Badgley Mischka, Balenciaga, Bob Mackie, C.D. Greene, Carlos Marquez, Carmen Marc Valvo, Chole, Debra Moises, Emanuel Ungaro, Eric Gaskins, Escada, Galanos, Gianfranco Ferre, Giorgio Armani, Holly Harp, Isabelle Kristensen, J.P. Todd, Jackie Rodgers, Jean-Louis Scherrer, Jean-Paul Gaultier, Jeannette Kastenberg, Lanvin, Manolo Blahnik, Marc Bouwer, Maria Dionyssiou, Maria Grachvogel, Mary McFadden, Moschino, New Republic, Paco Rabanne, Pamela Barrish, Pamela Dennis, Rifat Ozbek, Scott Hill for Donna Karan, Sophie Garel, Stephen Yearick, Todd Oldham, Vera Wang, Vestimenta, Vicky Tiel, Vivienne Tam, Zang Toi.

Evening Bags provided by Daniel Swarovski and Katherine Baumann.
Other evening bags by Fred Hayman Beverly Hills.

Eyewear by Kenneth Jay Lane and L.A. Eyeworks.

Jewelry by The House of Harry Winston.

Gift baskets courtesy of:
Bvlgari, Christofle Paris, Escada, Escada Sport, Flower Fashions, Fred Hayman Beverly Hills, Harry Winston, Hermes, Hush Puppies, Lladro, Piper Heidsieck Couvee Brut, Optical Shop of Aspen, Patron Tequila, Rosewood Hotels & Resorts, Salon Cristophe, The Spa at South Coast Plaza, Sulka, Swatch USA, Tea Tree Solutions, Thymes Limited, Tourneau, Wathne, Wolford.

To the Shrine Auditorium: Douglas Worthington, Auditorium Manager, Brian Fenske, Facility Manager.

The Academy gratefully acknowledges the cooperation of Hilton Hotels in arranging the accommodations for some of this evening's presenters, performers and nominees.

The Academy gratefully acknowledges the cooperation of United Airlines in arranging the transportation for some of this evening's presenters, performers and nominees.

Governors Ball and Pre-Show Cocktail Party catered by Wolfgang Puck in association with Restaurant Associates.

Ball decor by Ambrosia Productions featuring artist Hiro Yamagata.

Music provided by Jack Sheldon and the Jack Sheldon Orchestra and by the Chuck Wansley Band featuring Ellis Hall, Joy Burnworth and Gavin Christopher.

Governors Ball wines courtesy of Don and Rhonda Carano of Ferrari-Carano Vineyards and Winery.

Champagne presented by Laurent Perrier.

Pre-Show Cocktail Party wines presented by Baron Philippe de Rothschild.

Spirits courtesy of Absolut Citron.

Imported beer compliments of Heineken USA.

Fine ales and lagers compliments of Pyramid Breweries.

Water compliments of Evian Natural Spring Water and Ferrarelle Naturally Sparkling Water.

Governors Ball Coordination by Cheryl Cecchetto, Sequoia Productions.

## TELEVISION BROADCAST SPONSORED BY:
The American Express Company

AT&T
Chevrolet Motor Division
The Coca-Cola Company
Dannon Natural Spring Water
Eastman Kodak Company
IBM Corporation
JCPenney
M&M's Chocolate Candies
McDonald's
Pepperidge Farm Milano Cookies
PRIMESTAR Partners
Revlon
Serta, Inc.

## PROGRAM DESIGNED BY
Arnold & Isolde Schwartzman

Printing by
Newport Printing Systems

Oscar image based on the 69th Academy Awards poster designed by
Arnold Schwartzman

"Oscar" statuette ©AMPAS®

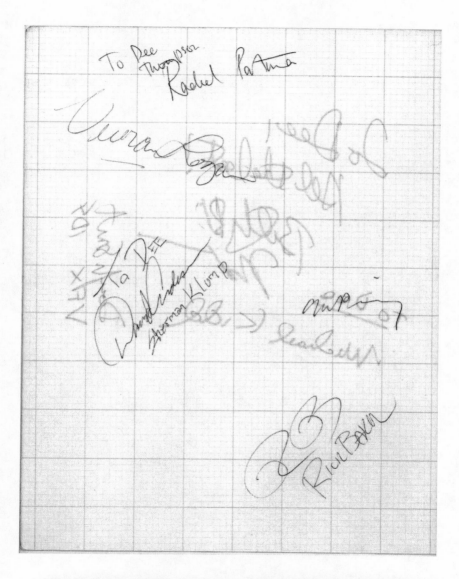

**AUTOGRAPHS FROM RICK BAKER, RACHEL PORTMAN
AND OTHERS**

**AUTOGRAPHS FROM MICHAEL KIDD, BILLY BOB THORNTON
& DOUGLAS SMITH**

**AUTOGRAPHS FROM MARIANNE JEAN-BAPTISTE AND NEW
FOUND FRIEND AND BROTHER—RAUL JULIA JR.**

# *TANTI TANTI GRAZI*
# *MANY, MANY THANKS*

I would like to thank first and foremost, **Almighty GOD** who made this event happen for me. Second, my mother, *Mrs. Evelyn Mable Thompson* who was my best friend, to whom I dedicate this book. She raised me from a child to a grown man and in doing that she always kept me and my other seven brothers and sisters in the church along the way. This loving nurturing woman turned all her kids over to **GOD** at a very young age and she continued to show us and demonstrate to us that there was a higher being who controlled all things and protected and guided us. **GOD** is the Alpha and the Omega, the Beginning and the End, the Bright and Morning Star. She taught me that with God on my side, who can be against me and to always put my trust in him. **Mrs. Evelyn Mable Thompson,** my mother, was well respected in the community. She demanded it. According to my loving Aunt Isabelle, "Eb (my mother's nick name), didn't play." I can remember when my mother was alive how she would introduce me to her friends. She'd say, "I'd like you to meet my movie star son, he works in the movie business out in Hollywood." I was sooo embarrassed by it. It would make me blush every time she would say it. Now, that she has gone on to heaven, I have sit and reflected on those moments. I can still hear her voice. I've said to myself, "Wow! She saw me as her successful Hollywood Movie Star," and if that was the case then now more than ever, I am so appreciative of that introduction. It just makes me feel good all over that I was that type of success in her eyes. To my ex-wife Deseree, who I grew up with, thanks Des. To all my children, Michael, Dwight, Amore' and Deshawn, you drive me in more ways than one, crazy sometimes but, I still love you. I love you all equally and want the very best for all of you. Thanks to my sisters and brothers who always have been a cheerleader for me and my career. They have always stood behind me, cheering me on and saying how successful I am and how **GOD** is going to take me higher and higher with my acting career. With this type of belief in me and support, I felt I couldn't do nothing but, be successful. They had so much faith in me and saw the success that I had become to them. To the rest of my family, friends, teachers and fellow actors, thank-you. I hope with this story it will reach someone, inspire and show them that all things are possible through faith and believing. For me, my faith and belief is in **GOD almighty**. Whatever you believe in, trust, pray and continue to believe and it will come to pass. **GOD** Bless and Good Will.


**DEE THOMPSON**